MY TAKE ON THE
SEVENTH DAY ADVENTIST CHURCH

Never Attend a Church That You Don't Check Out

By JIMMY B

The truth will make you free!
Where there is smoke there is fire!

xulon
PRESS

CONTENTS

PREFACE

Hopefully I have provided enough imformation to my readers to generate interest in my findings so they will look into the Seventh Day Adventist Church and its associated doctrine for themselves.

DEDICATION

I would like to dedicate this book to many, but one person in particular: my dear wife, Mary. Without her, this book would have never been written. I appreciate her so much because she not only married me, she has had to put up with me for nearly thirty-eight years.

Mary taught school for thirty-one years, and like me, always kept busy, yet she was and is always available to help me with my writing.

She always assisted me when I needed her and made sure she was always available. I would bounce my ideas and research off her before I would add my research and due-diligences' findings to my manuscript.

I want to make it clear that I also dedicate this book to those who assisted me in our twenty or so briefings and follow-up meetings. This is because there were so many who opened up to me when they discovered that I was for real, not being a Seventh Day Adventist. They were so helpful by telling it like it is in their individual Seventh Day Adventist churches. OK!

Again, I thank those who were and still are Seventh Day Adventist pastors and members, because it took much courage to stand up and say the things that they said, including the following: "I don't believe this or that about my church, and I have been told that I am not to depart the Seventh Day Adventist Church for any reason and that I am not even supposed to challenge their false prophetess nor can I tell others that I am saved."

I thank God for calling me and so many other volunteers who stepped up and gave of their time and money to right this wrong created by this church. ← I agree!

I Agree…

I agree!

ACKNOWLEDGMENTS

I want to thank Mark Martin, an exSeventh Day Adventist Pastor and many others, including those who called me with information without being solicited; for all their help in learning what is and what is not truthful in the SDA's church and their views and briefings on the Seventh Day Adventist Church.

CHAPTER 1

STARTED ATTENDING THE SDA CHURCH

About five years ago, I decided to change our family doctor. I had become disenchanted with the one that I had chosen about ten years ago.

When my wife and I began researching and asking around for a good doctor, I discovered one whom we eventually chose. I began to use him, and as I was told by others, he was friendly and appeared to be wonderful, and his staff also fit that description. All of his staff whom I met were friendly and professional, which helped me and my wife Mary select this particular doctor.

I had noticed a Seventh Day Adventist book or magazine in his office during one of my trips to see him and I asked about what they believed.

Not knowing anything about the Seventh Day Adventist Church, I assumed this church was the same as other churches with the exception that they attended church on Saturdays rather than Sundays.

This was interesting, and eventually my doctor told me that he led a Bible study in one of the local malls, and that he had rented a space for Bible studies because they were about to build a brand new church and volunteers had left their original church to help build this new church.

During one of our discussions during one of my appointments, my doctor informed me they needed someone to help them with music to kick off their Bible studies.

I had informed him that I was an old time musician and singer, and my wife also sang with me in spiritual concerts for churches or when we did church specials or concerts when we traveled in our RV.

After praying about it, I started to help out at the Bible studies, because I felt God called me to help out. So I would bring my guitar to the Bible studies on a regular basis, on Friday evenings. This continued for a number of months without incident, until in one of the Friday studies, my doctor mentioned a name of a woman whom he appeared to respect extremely. Being an old time reader and student of the Bible, I told him that I had never heard of her. Her name was Ellen G. White.

I was told this woman was highly respected in their church and that they even thought she was a prophetess.

Wow! I know the Bible well, but I had never heard of a woman named Ellen G. White.

I was flabbergasted and confused to find the Seventh Day Adventists claim her as their prophetess.

After the Bible study, I returned home to my wife. I must have been so surprised concerning what I had heard in that evening's Bible study, and it showed, because she ask me if there was anything wrong.

I informed her of what my doctor had said and I asked if she was aware of this Ellen G. White. She said she had never heard of her, because at that time she knew even less than I did concerning the Seventh Day Adventist Church.

I was somewhat surprised and became motivated in my soul to do some research and find out why the Seventh Day Adventist Church was given or had a prophetess of whom I had no knowledge. No one else I called and visited, including other pastors, didn't know about this so-called prophetess. My first thoughts were I might be involved with a cult of some type.

As time went along, my wife and I continued assisting with the music for the Bible studies and in the rented church they used on

Saturdays until their new church building was complete. I believe the church that they rented was part of the Church of God.

Naturally, Mary and I were exposed to many of the Seventh Day Adventist Bible studies and Sabbath schools and Sabbath day services, and we were blessed to get to know many of the Seventh Day Adventist people. We fell in love with many of the people, because at first we thought they respected our decision to be Nazarenes, but it wasn't long until we noticed some changes in meaning to the Bible to support their agenda. We became observers and gatherers of information about their teachings that were not biblical, including much of their church doctrine. We became even more concerned about their twenty-eight fundamental beliefs.

Many in the Church made attempts to recruit us (proselytize) and others from their home churches.

I felt called by God to help in music until the opening of the church. Keep in mind Mary and I attended our own church on Sundays. The reason that we attended the Seventh Day Adventist Church was to help out and assist where we were needed.

Apparently, God had called me to do what I was doing, because everything fell into place. Also from outside the church I could have never learned the intricacies and models of this arrogant church. Relating to their so-called "prophetess" my research found deceit, lies, and the church continued proselytizing.

Talking to many of their local and far away pastors and members in their church projected much confusion in the Seventh Day Adventist Church.

I was told by active Seventh Day Adventists that those who had departed the church did it willingly, and that they only had to fire few pastors and leaders in their church. I found this untrue. My research found there were many pastors and members that had departed the church. Later on I met many of those who had departed the SDA church because of their non-biblical doctrine and the fact that their church teaches the gospel plus Ellen G. White.

They tried to make me believe those who departed the church didn't depart because of their doctrine, but they departed mainly because of disagreements or something petty.

The reason I call this particular church arrogant is because they bragged to me and Mary that they are the only church with hope in these end times because the Seventh Day Adventist Church had been raised up by God and fine-tuned by their prophetess' writings and spoken word, because she was the spokesperson for God when she was alive and her writings were on the same level as the Bible.

They also said if I would read all of Ellen G. White's books and documents, I would learn the truth of the Bible and learn how close the Seventh Day Adventist Church was to God because of Ellen G. White's writings. They still used these writings, including her Sabbath school training literature, and in 1844, they became the remnant church of the end times. Nonsense abounds in this church when it come to the truths of the Bible and their dead "prophetess."

CHAPTER 2

THE SAGA CONTINUES

D ue to the SDA's musical needs, my wife and I felt we should help the church with their music. Not only did we play music for them, but we attended many of their Bible studies and services.

I would attend the SDA's Bible studies every week and sometimes twice a week. I would always make notes in my daily journal and ask questions, frequently challenging what they said or taught if it was not biblical or was questionable. This was when I discovered these people were so brainwashed by the false prophetess that they acted as if this woman was still alive, which makes me think the Seventh Day Adventist Church even has Satan's power of looking you in the eye and lying without flinching. It was weeks before I even knew Ellen G. White had died. That was how prevalent and powerful this woman was in their church.

This appears to be the catalyst of their power, because they can tell untruths so easily, which makes me think they believe the end justifies the means. I'm not sure everybody in the SDA church lies, but I do know they do lie about not proselytizing and how they feel about Ellen G. White. They made many efforts to recruit me and Mary into the SDA church, and they simply proselytized and/or made efforts to recruit me on a regular basis, including coming right out on more than one occasion and asking me to join their church. They continued trying to best me when I challenged their doctrine or their twenty-eight fundamental beliefs.

It was well known by nearly everyone in the new SDA church in this area that I did not believe in their dead false prophetess, nor did I believe in the things she said in her books and documents. The pastor of the new SDA church stopped by my office on numerous occasions to present the reasons why they believed in Ellen G. White and her writings. This was to no avail, because I knew the Bible as well as he did—if not better—and I would merrily tell him and others that all those references in her books and documents didn't prove a thing because they used her books and writings to try to challenge the Bible's truths. Challenging me gave me an incentive to expose the truths of their doctrines and beliefs.

I continued because I told them prior to finding out about their doctrine and Ellen G. White, plus I desired to gain knowledge to be able to make an informed decision to depart from them. Keep in mind I had made many friends with many of their pastors and members while we provided music for the churches. After I obtained my findings about the good and the bad and even the dangers of the Church, we stopped providing music and attending.

All that Ellen G. White nonsense that many in the church tried to make me believe didn't do anything for me other than make me more determined to not be pushed into reading non-biblical literature that someone said was dictated from God or the angels.

Every time I was given books or documents I noticed this church spent the majority of their time defending or covering up for her. What I saw and heard was a bunch of good people who had their heads in the sand and were blinded by lies and false teachings from their leadership and made-up fiction that had replaced the truth of the Bible.

Even today, the things that I observed bother me a little concerning how easily they presented their beliefs and arrogance to others, and how they could claim they believed something, but in reality, many in the church didn't.

These people believed Ellen G. White's writings and books plus they believe she should continue be their interpreter of the Bible.

Any scriptural meaning in the bible that she changed by her writings, whether in a book or in some other document, was all right because she said God had given her the authority to do so.

At this time I would like the readers' opinion: If you are a Seventh Day Adventist, are you being approached by God through the efforts of many who were called by God to research, perform due diligence, and investigate the Seventh Day Adventist Church? Many in the church are comparing their own church doctrine with the truths of the bible.

In many of my prayers, I prayed He would lead me to those of like mind so we could get all the Seventh Day Adventist nonsense over with.

I believe with all my heart that God is tired of all the confusion of a so-called church that doesn't even have a biblical doctrine.

This church also has twenty-eight fundamental beliefs, of which our research has proven only a few are biblical and this can be substantiated by comparing their twenty-eight fundamental beliefs. I provide a copy of them so the readers can compare for themselves with the Bible's truth

If someone other than a Seventh Day Adventist is reading this book, I believe you will also see and understand why God called our research group together to provide our findings in a book.

Hopefully, thousands of active Seventh Day Adventists will read and take to heart what we have written, because it is true and our research is well-founded and edited to make sense.

The findings of our research and due diligence will be hard to challenge because all one has to do is compare any of my findings within this book with the bible.

We went into this endeavor not thinking that it would take over five years to finish. However, keep in mind: God doesn't care about how hard something might be or how long it will take. He only cares we do what we are called to do. I know we will be blessed if we can pull just one Seventh Day Adventist from the fiery pits of hell. All our hard work will be worth it! What worries our research group is the challenge to get many SDAs to do the comparison between Ellen G. White's writings and the Bible's truths.

I have covertly asked many who are still active in the church, including pastors: What would you do if the Seventh Day Adventist Church dropped Ellen G. White?

You might be surprised what they answered. Many who were in the know said: "That could not happen because if Ellen G. White goes, the Seventh Day Adventist Church goes, because they wouldn't have her written doctrine, nor would they have many of their twenty-eight fundamental beliefs!"

My words: "In other words, without Ellen G. White's books, written doctrines the Seventh Day Adventists could not function."

Another answer was, "Without Ellen G. White, how could anyone get to heaven?"

Yet another answer was they didn't want to hear it, because without her, there would be no end time and everyone would parish.) Apparently this group had never read John 3:16 and many other scriptures that say differently.

Our group of Christian investigators prayed on a regular basis to ask God to help us spiritually as we researched and conducted our due-diligences, and we asked God to help us financially and make sure we did exactly what He desired us to do in our research.

It is hard to believe how God provided us the correct people to research the necessary items and topics and the funds for our research and books, and the costs to covertly obtain a large amount of information from Ellen G. White's estate, which guided our research and investigations.

CHAPTER 3

DOCTRINAL BELIEFS OF SEVENTH DAY ADVENTISTS

I must warn you that what I am about to write is true. The Seventh Day Adventists believe they are the real and only true end-times remnant church and the only remnant church and therefore people should depart their churches and join the Seventh Day Adventists.

I am presenting this church's doctrines and their twenty-eight fundamental beliefs. Read them for yourselves because I did. Talk about being brainwashed. I didn't find much to present that would make anyone a Seventh Day Adventist unless they had absolutely no understating of the real and true Bible.

The Seventh Day Adventists rely on people having little knowledge of the Bible. This makes it easy to fool people, especially telling newbies that their church is the only church and has a prophetess who talks to God and everybody else in heaven, including the angels.

Ellen G. White, who claimed to have "the spirit of prophecy," was an important early leader of the movement and taught a number of distinctive SDA's doctrines, including the Investigative Judgment and Sabbatarianism.

While the church's official theology now appears to be generally in the tradition of evangelical Christianity, certain SDA claims and unique doctrines continue to raise questions. These doctrines include the SDA belief that Sunday worship will result in the "Mark of the Beast," imbalanced teachings on keeping the commandments (baptism, Sabbath observance) that often imply a kind of salvation by works, the "remnant church" doctrine that implies the SDA is or will be God's only true church in the last days, and the doctrine of the Investigative Judgment.

Adventism:

Widespread trans-denominational movement inspired by William Miller's prediction or prophecy that Jesus' "advent" (return) would take place on October 22, 1843. This was Miller's first prophecy, but as we all know, Jesus didn't return. Of course this caused problems in the SDA church because many believed William Miller's prophecy. They were flabbergasted, irritated, and some were even surprised, according to our research. Many departed the church because his mistake or false prophecy let them down.

Yes, many good people had put their faith in William Miller the first time and crashed, and believe it or not, many continued putting their faith in William Miller and his second prediction of Christ's return, which was October 22, 1844. That also failed.

Yes, this was also a false prophecy, causing others to leave their church, and William Miller never tried predicting or prophesying again.

Even though William Miller never became a Seventh Day Adventist, he did have some part in the forming of the SDA church, but decided to continue being a Baptist.

Remember: Confusion ran deep in the early church and continues today.

Even after the Great Disappointment (the failed prophecy), many people in the movement continued to believe. Some suggested revised chronologies and new dates, eventually forming groups such as the Watchtower Bible and Tract Society. Others, notably Hiram Edson and Ellen G. White, told those in her day and time that the 1844 date was accurate, but that William Miller got the event wrong, because *according to Ellen G. White,* a heavenly (thus invisible) event had taken place. Their teachings became the basis of Seventh Day

Adventism, which eventually spawned its own offshoots, including Armstrongism, the Branch Davidians, and the Jehovah's Witnesses.

Actually, about this time, Ellen G. White began her career of lying; she started writing fiction and plagiarizing the books that she took credit for writing, without fear from the courts.

Generally, Sabbatarianism is the view that the Old Testament Sabbath commandment is to be observed unchanged by the church. As used in this context, Sabbatarian refers to an extreme form of the belief in which membership in the true church, or even salvation, is conditional upon keeping the Sabbath law. As such, Sabbatarian is, at the least, a form of legalism and at most a denial of salvation by grace. In most cases, the Jewish Sabbath (Saturday) must be observed by refraining from work, sports, and travel from sundown Friday evening to sundown Saturday evening. The belief is often accompanied by the observance of Jewish dietary laws and/or other Old Testament feasts.

Salvation by Grace:

The doctrine and message of the gospel that eternal life is not gained by or conditioned on works, but is an undeserved and free gift from God received through faith in Jesus Christ as the Lord and Savior who died for our sins and rose from the dead. Contrasted with salvation by works.

→ Investigative Judgment ← *Not biblical!*

One of the unique doctrines of the Seventh Day Adventist Church that make the placement of that church within evangelical Christianity questionable. First taught in Adventism by Hiram Edson, F.B. Hahn, and O.R.L. Crosier, it was accepted as "present truth" by those who would later become known as Seventh Day Adventists (SDAs) after it was confirmed and taught in visions received by Ellen G. White. The doctrine teaches in the Holy of Holies in the Heavenly Sanctuary, Christ is now conducting an investigation into the lives of all who have ever professed belief in Christ. He is judging all their works by the standard of God's law. All those whose lives fail to measure up to the standard of the law are rejected and condemned as not having true faith. Those whose lives meet that standard and thus manifest the perfect character and righteousness of Christ are recognized as having true faith, and so their sins are blotted out. SDAs say, this judgment vindicates the justice of God in saving those who believe in Jesus. It declares those who have remained loyal to God shall receive the kingdom. Evangelicals believe, and the Bible teaches (Romans 3:21–26), that God's justice in saving sinners who trust Jesus to save them is vindicated by the blood of Jesus—His death in their place, on their behalf.

Lies → Seventh Day Adventist Church Profile Unique Terms: "Investigative Judgment," "Spirit of Prophecy," "Coming into the Truth" (believing and living the full SDA message and lifestyle), "Remnant Church ← *Compared to the truths of the Bible this is fiction.*

History

William Miller, an itinerant, New England Baptist preacher predicted the end of the world and the Second Coming of Christ in 1844. Miller's followers condemned all the churches of the day as apostate and "Babylon," and warned Christians to come out of them. A great many did, and the "Adventist" movement was born and grew rapidly (Melton, J. Gordon, Encyclopedia of American Religions, Vol. 2, pp. 21–22). Christ did not appear in 1844. This was called the "Great Disappointment." Actually, their great disappointment was nothing more than someone who was a failed false prophet twice. Yes, not once, but twice. Seems to me this man was a double false prophet I wonder if the Seventh Day Adventist bunch knows the Bible used to stone false prophets because they were nothing but liars. Later on in the Bible, when a false prophet or prophetess was caught, we were told to simply ignore them and let them go away.

After this disappointment, one "little flock" still insisted the date of their original predictions had been correct. They decided the event marked by 1844 was not the Second Coming, but the entrance of Christ into the Holy of Holies in the Heavenly Sanctuary. There, they said, He began the "Investigative Judgment," which is not biblical! This doctrine was received and endorsed by Ellen G. White (Ibid., p. 680).

Attention: if the Bible doesn't support whatever someone is trying to teach you, it may be best to not believe it, because the Bible interprets the Bible.

Much more non-biblical claims Follows. *!*

The shut door doctrine is just more of Ellen G. White's fiction!

More Nonsense Follows!

From 1844 to 1851, the group taught the "shut door" doctrine, based on Jesus' parable of the ten virgins. Anyone who had not accepted the Adventist message by the time Jesus entered the Holy of Holies was to be shut out permanently, as were the five foolish virgins. Cut off from the Bridegroom, they could not join the Adventists or have any hope of eternal life. Ellen White not only approved and taught this doctrine, but her first vision experience was largely responsible for its being received by the Adventist group (Brinsmead, Robert, D., *Judged by the Gospel: A Review of Adventism*, pp. 130–33).

By 1846, the group had adopted the Seventh Day Baptists' view that the Saturday Sabbath must be observed by Christians. A highly elevated form of this doctrine, together with the doctrine of the Investigative Judgment, became the hallmarks of Seventh Day Adventism. In 1850, James and Ellen White began publishing a magazine, *The Review & Herald*, to disseminate Adventist and Sabbatarian doctrines. This helped many of the remaining "Millerites" to **coalesce into a distinctive body which adopted the name of Seventh Day Adventist Church in 1860, and formally incorporated in 1863**, with approximately 3,500 members in 125 congregations (Encyclopedia of American Religion, Vol. 2, p. 681).

Ellen White never held official title as the head of the church, but was one of its founders and acknowledged spiritual leader. She rather disingenuously declined to claim the title of "prophet," *calling herself a "messenger"* instead_(Damsteegt, P.G., et. al., Seventh-day Adventists Believe. . ., p. 224). *Yet, she claimed to have the "spirit* of prophecy," and that her messages were direct from God for the guidance and instruction of the church. With her knowledge and consent, others called her a prophet, and even "the Spirit of Prophecy" (Barnett, Maurice, *Ellen G. White & Inspiration*, pp. 5–17). Having only a third grade education, Ellen White said for years she was unable to read, bolstering the claim that her beautiful prose was inspired by God. However, it has been discovered she not only read, but *plagiarized other Christian authors throughout virtually all her writings.* The sad facts of this matter have been thoroughly and *indisputably established in several books* (see Rea, Walter, *The White Lie*; and *Judged by the Gospel*, pp. 361–83). Ellen White died in 1915 at age eighty-eight.

Historically, evangelicals have had difficulty defining and categorizing SDA. Much SDA doctrine is biblically orthodox. Within its ranks are many true Christians, some even in positions of prominence. At various points in its history, most notably in the 1888 General Conference, the SDA church has been shaken by the biblical gospel. In the 1970s, this became quite intense (See: Paxton, Geoffrey, J., *The Shaking of Adventism*). <u>Unfortunately, it produced</u> a polarization. The church administrators generally became more entrenched in the unorthodox positions of traditional SDA, while some pastors and even whole congregations left or were asked to leave the SDA church ("From Controversy to Crisis," *CRI Journal*, Vol. 11, No. 1, pp. 9–14). In official publications, the SDA church continues to defend Ellen White legends, and maintain there was no difference in the degree of inspiration she received from that received by Bible writers. All of the following are not biblical! (*Review & Herald*, 4 October 1928, p. 11; "Source of Final Appeal," *Adventist Review*, 3 June 1971, pp. 4–6; G. A. Irwin, Mark of the Beast, p. 1; "The Inspiration and Authority of the Ellen G. White's Writings," *Adventist Review,* 15 July 1982, p. 3; Ministry, October 1981, p. 8; see also, *Judged by the Gospel*, pp. 125–30). In their June 2000 General Conference, they voted to more aggressively affirm and support the "Spirit of Prophecy through the ministry of Ellen White" (*Adventist Today*, [online: July 2000]). They also teach a number of other doctrines clearly irreconcilable with the biblical gospel (see "Doctrine" below). So long as these things continue, evangelicals must persist in questioning the status of the SDA church organization in Christianity, and much more: the claim to be God's only true, end time "Remnant Church."

Folks, More of Ellen G. White's claims Follows!

The Sabbath: "[T]he divine institution of the Sabbath is to be restored ... The delivering of this message will precipitate a conflict that will involve the whole world. The central issue will be obedience to God's law and the observance of the Sabbath ... Those who reject it will eventually receive the mark of the beast" (Ibid., pp. 262–63). One of the SDA's study books.

In one of her most revered works, Ellen White wrote Sabbath observance would be the "line of distinction" in the "final test" that will separate God's end time people who "receive the seal of God" and are saved, from those who "receive the mark of the beast" (*The Great Controversy Between Christ and Satan*, p. 605).

Describing a supposed vision direct from God, Ellen White wrote, "I saw that the Holy Sabbath is, and will be, the separating wall between the true Israel of God and unbelievers" (*Early Writings*, p. 33). She added her emphasis relating to everything that she wrote and read. She also wrote of some Adventists failing to understand "Sabbath ... observance was of sufficient importance to draw a line between the people of God and unbelievers" (Ibid., p. 85).

If it is not of the Bible and doesn't agree with Bible truths, it is not biblically viable, period!

The Seventh Day Adventists continue to try to make people believe Ellen G. White's writings are from God, but this is one of the many things wrong with the Seventh Day Adventist, Ellen G. White's church.

After reading and studying this book, one must conclude the Ellen G. White Seventh Day Adventist Church teaches the gospel *plus* Ellen G. White!

I would call any church that uses writings that are not sanctioned by the Bible and God nothing more than a *cult*!

Ellen G. White was nothing more elegant than a lying, self-centered, plagiarizing false prophetess who completely ignored Revelation 22:18-19.

The Seventh Day Adventist Church, in their many actions, continue covering up both the Seventh Day Adventists' and Ellen G. White's lies, biblical contradictions, her extreme plagiarisms, and multitudes of her non-biblical antics!

Salvation by Works:

Any doctrine that denies salvation by grace alone, by teaching eternal life is merited, earned, conditioned, or maintained through human effort, religious ritual, financial donations, obedience to laws/commandments, church membership, and/or moral behavior.

CHAPTER 4

THE SDA'S TWENTY-EIGHT FUNDAMENTAL BELIEFS

Seventh-Day Adventists **tell us: Accept the Bible as their only creed** *and hold certain* **fundamental beliefs** *to be the teaching of the Holy Scriptures.*

Don't You Believe It!

The Seventh Day Adventists not only use Ellen G. White's writings and literature, they use many of her plagiarized books and her teaching material, and she has the final word in their churches. This document proves it!

Don't believe me? Ask anyone if they can or have attended one SDA church without hearing about Ellen G. White.

Ask the Seventh Day Adventists if they would even have a church without Ellen G. White. Take away Ellen G. White and the church has no woman-made doctrine and their twenty-eight fundamental beliefs are mostly not-biblical.

Keep this in mind any time a Seventh Day Adventist starts talking about worshiping on the Sabbath. We were told after assisting in the SDA's church for many months and prior to finding out the truth concerning the SDA church and their so-called prophetess that had died in 1915.

Reference: ***Deuteronomy 5:2-4:***

"The Lord our God made a covenant with us at Horeb. It was not with our ancestors that the Lord made this covenant, but with us, with all of us who are alive here to today. The Lord spoke to you face to face out of the fire on the mountain."

1. Holy Scriptures

The Holy Scriptures, Old and New Testaments, are the written Word of God, given by divine inspiration through holy men of God who spoke and wrote as they were moved by the Holy Spirit. In this Word, God has committed to man the knowledge necessary for salvation. The Holy Scriptures are the infallible revelation of His will. They are the standard of character, the test of experience, the authoritative revealer of doctrines, and the trustworthy record of God's acts in history (2 Peter 1:20, 21; 2 Timothy 3:16-17; Psalm 119:105; Proverbs 30:5-6; Isaiah 8:20; John 17:17; 1 Thessalonians 2:13; Hebrews 4:12).

2. Trinity

There is one God: Father, Son, and Holy Spirit, a unity of three co-eternal Persons. God is immortal, all-powerful, all-knowing, above all, and ever present. He is infinite and beyond human comprehension, yet known through His self-revelation. He is forever worthy of worship, adoration, and service by the whole creation (Deuteronomy 6:4; Matthew 28:19; 2 Corinthians 13:14; Ephesians 4:4-6; 1 Peter 1:2; 1 Timothy 1:17; Revelation 14:7).

3. Father

God the eternal Father is the Creator, Source, Sustainer, and Sovereign of all creation. He is just and holy, merciful and gracious, slow to anger, and abounding in steadfast love and faithfulness. The qualities and powers exhibited in the Son and the Holy Spirit are also revelations of the Father (Genesis 1:1; Revelation 4:11; 1

Corinthians 15:28; John 3:16; 1 John 4:8; 1 Timothy 1:17; Exodus 34:6-7; John 14:9).

4. Son

God the eternal Son became incarnate in Jesus Christ. Through Him, all things were created, the character of God is revealed, the salvation of humanity is accomplished, and the world is judged. Forever truly God, He became also truly man, Jesus the Christ. He was conceived of the Holy Spirit and born of the virgin Mary. He lived and experienced temptation as a human being, but perfectly exemplified the righteousness and love of God. By His miracles He manifested God's power and was attested as God's promised Messiah. He suffered and died voluntarily on the cross for our sins and in our place, was raised from the dead, and ascended to minister in the heavenly sanctuary on our behalf. He will come again in glory for the final deliverance of His people and the restoration of all things (John 1:1-3, 14; Colossians 1:15-19; John 10:30, 14:9; Romans 6:23; 2 Corinthians 5:17-19; John 5:22; Luke 1:35; Philippians 2:5-11; Hebrews 2:9-18; 1 Corinthians 15:3-4; Hebrews 8:1-2; John 14:1-3).

5. Holy Spirit

God the eternal Spirit was active with the Father and the Son in creation, incarnation, and redemption. He inspired the writers of Scripture. He filled Christ's life with power. He draws and convicts human beings; and those who respond, He renews and transforms into the image of God. Sent by the Father and the Son to be always with His children, He extends spiritual gifts to the church, empowers it to bear witness to Christ, and in harmony with the Scriptures, leads it into all truth (Genesis 1:1-2; Luke 1:35, 4:18; Acts 10:38; 2 Peter 1:21; 2 Corinthians 3:18; Ephesians 4:11-12; Acts 1:8; John 14:16-18, 26, 15:26-27, 16:7-13).

6. Creation

God is Creator of all things, and has revealed in Scripture the authentic account of His creative activity. In six days, the Lord made "the heavens and the earth" and all living things upon the earth, and rested on the seventh day of that first week. Thus He established the Sabbath as a perpetual memorial of His completed creative work. The first man and woman were made in the image of God as the crowning work of creation, given dominion over the world, and charged with responsibility to care for it. When the world was finished, it was "very good," declaring the glory of God (Genesis 1, 2; Exodus 20:8-11; Psalm 19:1-6, 33:6, 9; 104; Hebrews 11:3).

7. Nature of Man

Man and woman were made in the image of God with individuality, the power, and freedom to think and to do. Though created free beings, each is an indivisible unity of body, mind, and spirit, dependent upon God for life and breath and all else. When our first parents disobeyed God, they denied their dependence upon Him and fell from their high position under God. The image of God in them was marred and they became subject to death. Their descendants share this fallen nature and its consequences. They are born with weaknesses and tendencies to evil. Yet, God in Christ reconciled the world to Himself and by His Spirit restores in penitent mortals the image of their Maker. Created for the glory of God, they are called to love Him and one another, and to care for their environment (Genesis 1:26-28, 2:7, 15; Psalm 8:4-8, 51:5,10; Acts 17:24-28; Genesis 3; Romans 5:12-17; 2 Corinthians 5:19-20; 1 John 4:7-8, 11, 20).

8. Great Controversy

All humanity is now involved in a great controversy between Christ and Satan regarding the character of God, His law, and His sovereignty over the universe. This conflict originated in heaven when a created being, endowed with freedom of choice, in self-exaltation became Satan, God's adversary, and led into rebellion a portion of the angels. He introduced the spirit of rebellion into this world when he led Adam and Eve into sin. This human sin resulted in the distortion of the image of God in humanity, the disordering of the created world, and its eventual devastation at the time of the world-wide flood. Observed by the whole creation, this world became the arena of the universal conflict, out of which the God of love will ultimately be vindicated. To assist His people in this controversy, Christ sends the Holy Spirit and the loyal angels to guide, protect, and sustain them in the way of salvation (Revelation 12:4-9; Isaiah 14:12-14; Ezekiel 28:12-18; Genesis 3, 6-8; Romans 1:19-32; 5:12-21; 8:19-22; 2 Peter 3:6; 1 Corinthians 4:9; Hebrews 1:14).

9. Life, Death, and Resurrection of Christ

In Christ's life of perfect obedience to God's will, His suffering, death, and resurrection, God provided the only means of atonement for human sin, so that those who by faith accept this atonement may have eternal life, and the whole creation may better understand the infinite and holy love of the Creator. This perfect atonement vindicates the righteousness of God's law and the graciousness of His character; for it both condemns our sin and provides for our forgiveness. The death of Christ is substitutionary and expiatory, reconciling and transforming. The resurrection of Christ proclaims God's triumph over the forces of evil, and for those who accept the atonement assures their final victory over sin and death. It declares the Lordship of Jesus Christ, before whom every knee in heaven and on earth will bow (John 3:16; Isaiah 53; 1 Peter 2:21-22; 1 Corinthians 15:3-4, 20-22; 2 Corinthians 5:14-15, 19-21; Romans 1:4; 3:25; 4:25, 8:3-4; 1 John 2:2, 4:10; Colossians 2:15; Philippians 2:6-11).

10. Experience of Salvation

In infinite love and mercy, God made Christ, who knew no sin, to be sin for us, so that in Him we might be made in the righteousness of God. Led by the Holy Spirit, we sense our need, acknowledge our sinfulness, repent of our transgressions, and exercise faith in Jesus as Lord and Christ, as substitute and example. This faith which receives salvation comes through the divine power of the Word and is the gift of God's grace. Through Christ we are justified, adopted as God's sons and daughters, and delivered from the lordship of sin. Through the Spirit we are born again and sanctified; the Spirit renews our minds, writes God's law of love in our hearts, and we are given the power to live a holy life. Abiding in Him, we become partakers of the divine nature and have the assurance of salvation now and in the judgment (2 Corinthians 5:17-21; John 3:16; Galatians 1:4, 4:4-7, 3:13-14, 26; Titus 3:3-7, John 3:3-8, 16:8; 1 Peter 1:23, 2:21-22; Romans 10:17, 3:21-26, 5:6-10, 8:1-4,14-17, 12:2; Luke 17:5; Mark 9:23-24; Ephesians 2:5-10; Colossians 1:13-14; Hebrews 8:7-12; Ezekiel 36:25-27; 2 Peter 1:3-4).

11. Growing in Christ

By His death on the cross, Jesus triumphed over the forces of evil. He who subjugated the demonic spirits during His earthly ministry has broken their power and made certain their ultimate doom. Jesus' victory gives us victory over the evil forces that still seek to control us, as we walk with Him in peace, joy, and assurance of His love. Now the Holy Spirit dwells within us and empowers us. Continually committed to Jesus as our Savior and Lord, we are set free from the burden of our past deeds. No longer do we live in the darkness, fear of evil powers, ignorance, and meaninglessness of our former way of life. In this new freedom in Jesus, we are called to grow into the likeness of His character, communing with Him daily in prayer, feeding on His Word, meditating on it and on His providence, singing His praises, gathering together for worship, and participating in the mission of the church. As we give ourselves in loving service to those around us and in witnessing to His salvation, His constant presence with us through the Spirit transforms every moment and every task into a spiritual experience (Psalm 1:1,-2; 23:4; 77:11-12; Colossians 1:13-14, 2:6, 14-15; Luke 10:17-20; Ephesians 5:19-20, 6:12-18; 1 Thessalonians 5:23; 2 Peter 2:9, 3:18; 2 Corinthians 3:17-18; Philippians 3:7-14; 1 Thessalonians 5:16-18; Matthew 20:25-28; John 20:21; Galatians 5:22-25; Romans 8:38-39; 1 John 4:4; Hebrews 10:25).

12. Church

The church is the community of believers who confess Jesus Christ as Lord and Savior. In continuity with the people of God in Old Testament times, we are called out from the world; and we join together for worship, for fellowship, for instruction in the Word, for the celebration of the Lord's Supper, for service to all mankind, and for the worldwide proclamation of the gospel. The church derives its authority from Christ, who is the incarnate Word, and from the Scriptures, which are the written Word. The church is God's family; adopted by Him as children, its members live on the basis of the new covenant. The church is the body of Christ, a community of faith of which Christ Himself is the Head. The church is the bride for whom Christ died that He might sanctify and cleanse her. At His return in triumph, He will present her to Himself a glorious church, the faithful of all the ages, the purchase of His blood, not having spot or wrinkle, but holy and without blemish (Genesis 12:3; Acts 7:38; Ephesians 1:22-23, 2:19-22, 3:8-11, 4:11-15, 5:23-27; Matthew 28:19-20, 16:13-20,,18:18; Colossians 1:17-18).

13. Remnant and Its Mission

The universal church is composed of all who truly believe in Christ, but in the last days, a time of widespread apostasy, a remnant has been called out to keep the commandments of God and the faith of Jesus. This remnant announces the arrival of the judgment hour, proclaims salvation through Christ, and heralds the approach of His second advent. This proclamation is symbolized by the three angels of Revelation 14; it coincides with the work of judgment in heaven and results in a work of repentance and reform on earth. Every believer is called to have a personal part in this worldwide witness (Revelation 12:17, 14:6-12, 18:1-4, 21:1-14; 2 Corinthians 5:10; Jude 3, 14; 1 Peter 1:16-19; 2 Peter 3:10-14).

14. Unity in the Body of Christ

The church is one body with many members, called from every nation, kindred, tongue, and people. In Christ, we are a new creation; distinctions of race, culture, learning, and nationality, and differences between high and low, rich and poor, male and female, must not be divisive among us. We are all equal in Christ, who by one Spirit has bonded us into one fellowship with Him and with one another; we are to serve and be served without partiality or reservation. Through the revelation of Jesus Christ in the Scriptures, we share the same faith and hope, and reach out in one witness to all. This unity has its source in the oneness of the triune God, who has adopted us as His children (Romans 12:4-5; 1 Corinthians 12:12-14; Matthew 28:19-20; Psalm 133:1; 2 Corinthians 5:16-17; Acts 17:26-27; Galatians 3:27, 29; Colossians 3:10-15; Ephesians 4:1-6, 14-16; John 17:20-23).

15. Baptism

By baptism we confess our faith in the death and resurrection of Jesus Christ, and testify of our death to sin and of our purpose to walk in newness of life. Thus we acknowledge Christ as Lord and Savior, become His people, and are received as members by His church. Baptism is a symbol of our union with Christ, the forgiveness of our sins, and our reception of the Holy Spirit. It is by immersion in water and is contingent on an affirmation of faith in Jesus and evidence of repentance of sin. It follows instruction in the Holy Scriptures and acceptance of their teachings. *They also ask you accept and believe Ellen G. White's writings!* (Romans 6:1-6; Colossians 2:12-13; Acts 16:30-33, 22:16, 2:38; Matthew 28:19-20).

16. Lord's Supper

The Lord's Supper is a participation in the emblems of the body and blood of Jesus as an expression of faith in Him, our Lord and Savior. In this experience of communion, Christ is present to meet and strengthen His people. As we partake, we joyfully proclaim the Lord's death until He comes again. Preparation for the Supper includes self-examination, repentance, and confession. The Master ordained the service of foot washing to signify renewed cleansing, to express a willingness to serve one another in Christ-like humility, and to unite our hearts in love. The communion service is open to all believing Christians (1 Corinthians 10:16-17; 11:23-30; Matthew 26:17-30; Revelation 3:20; John 6:48-63; 13:1-17).

17. Spiritual Gifts and Ministries

God bestows upon all members of His church in every age spiritual gifts, which each member is to employ in loving ministry for the common good of the church and of humanity. Given by the agency of the Holy Spirit, who apportions to each member as He wills, the gifts provide all abilities and ministries needed by the church to fulfill its divinely ordained functions. According to the Scriptures, these gifts include such ministries as faith, healing, prophecy, proclamation, teaching, administration, reconciliation, compassion, and self-sacrificing service and charity for the help and encouragement of people. Some members are called of God and endowed by the Spirit for functions recognized by the church in pastoral, evangelistic, apostolic, and teaching ministries particularly needed to equip the members for service, to build up the church to spiritual maturity, and to foster unity of the faith and knowledge of God. When members employ these spiritual gifts as faithful stewards of God's varied grace, the church is protected from the destructive influence of false doctrine, grows with a growth that is from God, and is built up in faith and love (Romans 12:4-8; 1 Corinthians 12:9-11, 27-28; Ephesians 4:8, 11-16; Acts 6:1-7; 1 Timothy 3:1-13; 1 Peter 4:10-11).

18. The Gift of Prophecy

One of the gifts of the Holy Spirit is prophecy. This gift is an identifying mark of the remnant church and was manifested in the ministry of Ellen G. White. As the Lord's messenger, her writings are a continuing and authoritative source of truth, which provides for the church comfort, guidance, instruction, and correction. **They also make clear the Bible is the standard by which all teaching and**

experience must be tested. (Joel 2:28-29; Acts 2:14-21; Hebrews 1:1-3; Revelation 12:17, 19:10.)

19. Law of God

The great principles of God's law are embodied in the Ten Commandments and exemplified in the life of Christ. They express God's love, will, and purposes concerning human conduct and relationships and are binding upon all people in every age. These precepts are the basis of God's covenant with His people and the standard in God's judgment. Through the agency of the Holy Spirit, they point out sin and awaken a sense of need for a Savior. Salvation is all of grace and not of works, but its fruitage is obedience to the Commandments. This obedience develops Christian character and results in a sense of well-being. It is evidence of our love for the Lord and our concern for our fellow men. The obedience of faith demonstrates the power of Christ to transform lives, and therefore strengthens Christian witness (Exodus 20:1-17; Psalm 19:7-14; 40:7-8; Matthew 5:17-20, 22:36-40; Deuteronomy 28:1-14; Hebrews 8:8-10; John 15:7-10; Ephesians 2:8-10; 1 John 5:3; Romans 8:3-4).

20. Sabbath

The beneficent Creator, after the six days of Creation, rested on the seventh day and instituted the Sabbath for all people as a memorial of Creation. The fourth commandment of God's unchangeable law requires the observance of this seventh day Sabbath as the day of rest, worship, and ministry in harmony with the teaching and practice of Jesus, the Lord of the Sabbath. The Sabbath is a day of delightful communion with God and one another. **It is a symbol of our redemption in Christ, a sign of our sanctification, a token of our allegiance, and a foretaste of our eternal future in God's kingdom. The Sabbath is God's perpetual sign of His eternal covenant between Him and His people**. Joyful observance of this holy time from evening to evening, sunset to sunset, is a celebration of God's creative and redemptive acts (Genesis 2:1-3; Exodus 20:8-11, 31:13-17; Luke 4:16; Isaiah 56:5-6, 58:13-14; Matthew 12:1-12;

Ezekiel 20:12, 20; Deuteronomy 5:12-15; Hebrews 4:1-11; Leviticus 23:32; Mark 1:32).

21. Stewardship

We are God's stewards, entrusted by Him with time and opportunities, abilities and possessions, and the blessings of the earth and its resources. We are responsible to Him for their proper use. We acknowledge God's ownership by faithful service to Him and our fellow men, and by returning tithes and giving offerings for the proclamation of His gospel and the support and growth of His church. Stewardship is a privilege given to us by God for nurture in love and the victory over selfishness and covetousness. The steward rejoices in the blessings that come to others as a result of his faithfulness (Genesis 1:26-28, 2:15; 1 Chronicles 29:14; Haggai 1:3-11; Malachi 3:8-12; 1 Corinthians 9:9-14; Matthew 23:23; 2 Corinthians 8:1-15; Romans 15:26-27).

22. Christian Behavior

We are called to be a godly people who think, feel, and act in harmony with the principles of heaven. For the Spirit to recreate in us the character of our Lord, we involve ourselves only in those things which will produce Christ-like purity, health, and joy in our lives. This means our amusement and entertainment should meet the highest standards of Christian taste and beauty. While recognizing cultural differences, our dress is to be simple, modest, and neat, befitting those whose true beauty does not consist of outward adornment, but in the imperishable ornament of a gentle and quiet spirit. It also means because our bodies are the temples of the Holy Spirit, we are to care for them intelligently. Along with adequate exercise and rest, we are to adopt the most healthful diet possible and abstain from the unclean foods identified in the Scriptures. Since alcoholic beverages, tobacco, and the irresponsible use of drugs and narcotics are harmful to our bodies, we are to abstain from them as well. Instead, we are to engage in whatever brings our thoughts and bodies into the discipline of Christ, who desires our wholesomeness, joy, and goodness

(Romans 12:1-2; 1 John 2:6; Ephesians 5:1-21; Philippians 4:8; 2 Corinthians 10:5; 6:14-7:1; 1 Peter 3:1-4; 1 Corinthians 6:19-20; 10:31; Leviticus 11:1-47; 3 John 2).

23. *Marriage and the Family*

Marriage was divinely established in Eden and affirmed by Jesus to be a lifelong union between a man and a woman in loving companionship. For the Christian, a marriage commitment is to God as well as to the spouse, and should be entered into only between partners who share a common faith. Mutual love, honor, respect, and responsibility are the fabric of this relationship, which is to reflect the love, sanctity, closeness, and permanence of the relationship between Christ and His church. Regarding divorce, Jesus taught that the person who divorces a spouse, except for fornication, and marries another, commits adultery. Although some family relationships may fall short of the ideal, marriage partners who fully commit themselves to each other in Christ may achieve loving unity through the guidance of the Spirit and the nurture of the church. God blesses the family and intends that its members shall assist each other toward complete maturity. Parents are to bring up their children to love and obey the Lord. By their example and their words, they are to teach them that Christ is a loving disciplinarian, ever tender and caring, who wants them to become members of His body, the family of God. Increasing family closeness is one of the earmarks of the final gospel message. (Genesis 2:18-25; Matthew 5:31-32, 19:3-9; John 2:1-11; 2 Corinthians 6:14; Ephesians 5:21-33, 6:1-4; Mark 10:11-12; Luke 16:18; 1 Corinthians 7:10-11; Exodus 20:12; Deuteronomy 6:5-9; Proverbs 22:6; Malachi 4:5-6).

24. *Christ's Ministry in the Heavenly Sanctuary* ß ***Not biblical!***

There is a sanctuary in heaven, the true tabernacle, which the Lord set up and not man. In it, Christ ministers on our behalf, making available to believers the benefits of His atoning sacrifice offered once for all on the cross. He was inaugurated as our great High Priest and began His intercessory ministry at the time of His ascension. In

1844, at the end of the prophetic period of 2,300 days, He entered the second and last phase of His atoning ministry. It is a work of investigative judgment, which is part of the ultimate disposition of all sin, typified by the cleansing of the ancient Hebrew sanctuary on the Day of Atonement. In that typical service, the sanctuary was cleansed with the blood of animal sacrifices, but the heavenly things are purified with the perfect sacrifice of the blood of Jesus. The investigative judgment reveals to heavenly intelligences who among the dead are asleep in Christ and therefore, in Him, are deemed worthy to have part in the first resurrection. It also makes manifest who among the living are abiding in Christ, keeping the commandments of God and the faith of Jesus, and in Him, therefore, are ready for translation into His everlasting kingdom. This judgment vindicates the justice of God in saving those who believe in Jesus. It declares those who have remained loyal to God shall receive the kingdom. The completion of this ministry of Christ will mark the close of human probation (***doesn't say this in the Bible***) before the Second Advent (Hebrews 8:1-5, 4:14-16, 9:11-28, 10:19-22, 1:3, 2:16-17; Daniel 7:9-27, 8:13-14, 9:24-27; Numbers 14:34; Ezekiel 4:6; Leviticus 16; Revelation 14:6-7, 20:12, 14:12, 22:12).

25. Second Coming of Christ

The second coming of Christ is the blessed hope of the church, the grand climax of the gospel. The Savior's coming will be literal, personal, visible, and worldwide. When He returns, the righteous dead will be resurrected, and together with the righteous living will be glorified and taken to heaven, but the unrighteous will die. The almost complete fulfillment of most lines of prophecy, together with the present condition of the world, indicates that Christ's coming is imminent. The time of that event has not been revealed, and we are therefore exhorted to be ready at all times (Titus 2:13; Hebrews 9:28; John 14:1-3; Acts 1:9-11; Matthew 24; Revelation 1:7, 14:14-20; 19:11-21; 1 Thessalonians 4:13-18, 5:1-6; 1 Corinthians 15:51-54; 2 Thessalonians 1:7-10, 2:8; Mark 13; Luke 21; 2 Timothy 3:1-5).

26. Death and Resurrection

The wages of sin is death. However, God, who alone is immortal, will grant eternal life to His redeemed. Until that day, death is an unconscious state for all people. When Christ, who is our life, appears, the resurrected righteous and the living righteous will be glorified and caught up to meet their Lord. The second resurrection, the resurrection of the unrighteous, will take place a thousand years later (Romans 6:23; 1 Timothy 6:15-16; Ecclesiastes 9:5-6; Psalm 146:3-4; John 5:28-29, 11:11-14; Colossians 3:4; 1 Corinthians 15:51-54; 1 Thessalonians 4:13-17; Revelation 20:1-10).

27. Millennium and the End of Sin

The millennium is the thousand-year reign of Christ with His saints in heaven between the first and second resurrections. During this time, the wicked dead will be judged; the earth will be utterly desolate, without living human inhabitants, but occupied by Satan and his angels. At its close, Christ with His saints and the Holy City will descend from heaven to earth. The unrighteous dead will then be resurrected, and with Satan and his angels will surround the city; but fire from God will consume them and cleanse the earth. The universe will thus be freed of sin and sinners forever (Revelation 20, 21:1-15; 1 Corinthians 6:2-3; Jeremiah 4:23-26; Malachi 4:1; Ezekiel 28:18-19.).

28. New Earth

On the new earth, in which righteousness dwells, God will provide an eternal home for the redeemed and a perfect environment for everlasting life, love, joy, and learning in His presence. For here God Himself will dwell with His people, and suffering and death will have passed away. The great controversy will be ended, and sin will be no more. All things, animate and inanimate, will declare God is love; and He shall reign forever. Amen. (2 Peter 3:13; Isaiah 35; 65:17-25; Matthew 5:5; Revelation 21:1-7, 22:1-5, 11:15)

Please study these, and you will find most of the Seventh Day Adventists' doctrines and most of their twenty-eight fundamental beliefs are not supported by the Bible, but their doctrines and fundamental beliefs are supported by the fiction writings of Ellen G. White, a proven false prophetess.

They spend most of their time trying to cover up their past association with the Jehovah's Witnesses and William Miller, a man with a plan to take information from the book of Daniel and calculate a date of the return of Jesus.

CHAPTER 5

ELLEN. G. WHITE'S BIBLE CONTRADICTIONS

Fifty-three Bible contradictions are plenty for someone who kept saying she was more than just a woman like any other woman. She continued to elevate herself with only her spoken words and her writings, and believe me, her writings only confused the church and spread her non-biblical doctrines, and most of their twenty-eight fundamental beliefs are also not biblical.

The fifty-three known contradictions between Ellen G. White's Seventh Day Adventist teachings and the truth of the Bible:

1. Was the plan of salvation made after the fall?
2. Was Adam with Eve when she was tempted in the garden?
3. Was Adam deceived by Satan?
4. Who spoke to Cain?
5. Did pre-flood humans mate with animals and give birth to new sub-human species and races?
6. Did God or an angel shut the door of Noah's Ark?
7. Was the Tower of Babel built before the Flood?
8. Was the Tower of Babel built to escape another flood?
9. Was Moses' wife, Zipporah, a Cushite?
10. Were the Israelites destroyed by gluttony?

11. Did God send ravens to feed Elijah?
12. Did Samson disobey God when he married a Philistine?
13. Did the high priest carry the blood of sacrificed animals into the holy place each day?
14. Did Christ resemble other children?
15. Was the man Jesus Christ also truly God?
16. While tempting Jesus, did Satan claim to be the angel who had saved Isaac from certain death?
17. Who chose Judas to be one of Jesus' twelve disciples?
18. Did dogs eat Judas' remains?
19. Did Herod place a tattered robe on Jesus?
20. Did Jesus faint three times under the Cross?
21. Did Satan tempt Christ after He fasted forty days?
22. Was Mary led away from the scene and Jesus' bones broken during His crucifixion?
23. Did Jesus' humanity and divinity die on the Cross?
24. Did Jesus die to give us a second probation?
25. Was the atonement for sin completed at the Cross?
26. Does the blood of Christ cancel sin?
27. Are confessed sins transferred to the heavenly sanctuary by the blood of Christ?
28. Who bears our sins?
29. Does God require a trespass offering before He pardons us?
30. Can we say we are saved right now by Christ's grace?
31. Can the faith of believing parents save their children?
32. Will the sins of the slave be transferred to the slave master?
33. Can ignorant slaves be saved?
34. Can we legitimately say, "I have ceased to sin"?
35. Will obeying The Commandments earn me God's favor?
36. Do our obedience and faith reconcile us to God?
37. As a Christian, do I still stand condemned before God?
38. Must I be perfect before Christ will accept me?
39. Did Jesus enter the most holy place of the heavenly temple before October 22, 1844?
40. Are the forgiven sins of the saints not blotted out until the Great Day of Final Reward?
41. Did Paul learn the Gospel from men in the church?

42. What is "The Seal of God"?
43. Are we required to kneel every time we pray?
44. Will people be lost because their pastor is untidy?
45. Is it a sin to be sick?
46. Will God prevent the wicked from killing his people who refuse to receive the mark of the beast?
47. Do the wicked try to repent as they experience The Seven Last Plagues?
48. Can Satan answer prayers directed to God?
49. Will we know the exact day and hour of Christ's Second Coming?
50. Does Jesus return to Earth at the stroke of midnight?
51. Will the saved have wings in the Resurrection?
52. Could Jesus see through the portals of the tomb?
53. Did Enoch think to save Sodom?

Origins of the known contradictions of which Ellen G. White was guilty as follows:

We advise the reader to claim John 16:13 ("Howbeit when He, the Spirit of truth, is come, He will guide you into all truth") as you go over this list.

All quotes and writings from both Ellen White and the Bible are shown here exactly as they appear in the original documents.

The truth will make you free!

The Fifty-three Questions:

1. Was the plan of salvation made after the fall?

EGW: **Yes.** "The kingdom of grace was instituted immediately after the fall of man, when a plan was devised for the redemption of the guilty race" (*Great Controversy,* p. 347).

BIBLE: **No.**

For you know that it was not with perishable things such as silver or gold that you were redeemed from the empty way of life handed down to you from your forefathers, but with the precious blood of

Christ, a lamb without blemish or defect. He was chosen before the creation of the world, but was revealed in these last times for your sake. (1 Peter 1:18-20)

> "For he chose us in him before the creation of the world to be holy and blameless in his sight" (Ephesians 1:4).

2. Was Adam with Eve when she was tempted in the Garden?

EGW: **No.**

> The angels had cautioned Eve to beware of separating herself from her husband while occupied in their daily labor in the garden; with him she would be in less temptation than if she were alone. But absorbed in her pleasing task, she unconsciously wandered from his side. On perceiving that she was alone, she felt an apprehension of danger. ... She soon found herself gazing with mingled curiosity and admiration upon the forbidden tree. (*Patriarchs and Prophets*, pp. 53, 54).

BIBLE: **Yes.** "When the woman saw that the fruit of the tree was good for food and pleasing to the eye, and also desirable for gaining wisdom, she took some and ate it. She also gave some to her husband, who was with her, and he ate it" (Genesis 3:6).

3. Was Adam deceived by Satan?

EGW: **Yes**. "Satan, who is the father of lies, deceived Adam in a similar way, telling him that he need not obey God, that he would not die if he transgressed the law" (*Evangelism*, p. 598).

BIBLE: **No.** "And Adam was not the one deceived; it was the woman who was deceived and became a sinner" (1 Timothy 2:14).

4. Who spoke to Cain?

EGW: **An angel.** "Through an angel messenger the divine warning was conveyed: 'If thou doest well, shalt thou not be accepted?'" (*Patriarchs and Prophets*, p. 74)

BIBLE: **The Lord.** "Then the Lord said to Cain, 'Why are you angry? Why is your face downcast? If you do what is right will you not be accepted?' ... So Cain went out from the Lord's presence" (Genesis 4:6-7, 10, 13, 15-16).

5. Did pre-flood humans mate with animals and give birth to new sub-human species and races?

EGW: **Yes.** "But if there was one sin above another which called for the destruction of the race by the flood, it was the base crime of amalgamation of man and beast which defaced the image of God, and caused confusion everywhere" (*Spiritual Gifts*, vol. 3, p. 64). This is more of the SDA's so-called prophetess continuing to make things up and add words to the Bible for her own agenda.

> Every species of animal which God had created were preserved in the ark. The confused species which God did not create, which were the result of amalgamation, were destroyed by the flood. Since the flood there has been amalgamation of man and beast, as may be seen in the almost endless varieties of species of animals, and in certain races of men. (*Spiritual Gifts*, vol. 3, p. 75)

BIBLE: **No.**

> And God said, "Let the land produce living creatures according to their kinds: livestock, creatures that move long the ground, and wild animals, each according to its kind." And it was so. God made the wild animals according to their kinds, the livestock according to their kinds, and all the creatures that

move along the ground according to their kinds. And God saw that it was good. (Genesis 1:24, 25)

6. Did God or an angel shut the door of Noah's Ark?

EGW: **Angel.** "An angel is seen by the scoffing multitude descending from heaven clothed with brightness like the lightning. He closes that massive outer door, and takes his course upward to heaven again" (*Spiritual Gifts*, vol. 3, p. 68, written in 1864).

EGW: **God.** "God had shut it, and God alone could open it" (*Patriarchs and Prophets*, p. 98, written in 1890).

BIBLE: **God.** "Then the Lord shut him in" (Genesis 7:16).

7. Was the Tower of Babel built before The Flood?

EGW: **Yes.** "This system was corrupted before the flood by those who separated themselves from the faithful followers of God, and engaged in the building of the tower of Babel" (*Spiritual Gifts,* vol. 3, p. 301).

BIBLE: **No.** "After the Flood ... they said, 'Come, let us build ourselves a city, with a tower that reaches to the heavens, so that we may make a name for ourselves and not be scattered over the face of the whole earth'" (Genesis 9:28 and 11:4).

8. Was the Tower of Babel built to escape another flood?

EGW: **Yes.**

> The dwellers on the plain of Shinar disbelieved God's covenant that He would not again bring a flood upon the earth. Many of them denied the existence of God and attributed the Flood to the operation of natural causes. ... One object before them in the erection of the tower was to secure their own safety in case of another deluge. By carrying the structure to a much greater height than was reached by the waters of the

Flood, they thought to place themselves beyond all possibility of danger. And as they would be able to ascend to the region of the clouds, they hoped to ascertain the cause of the Flood. (*Patriarchs and Prophets*, p. 119)

BIBLE: **No.** "Then they said, 'Come, let us build ourselves a city, with a tower that reaches to the heavens, so that we may make a name for ourselves and not be scattered over the face of the whole earth'" (Genesis 11:4).

9. Was Moses' wife Zipporah a Cushite?

EGW: **Yes.** "[Miriam] complained of Moses because he married an Ethiopian (Cushite) woman" (*Spiritual Gifts*, vol. 4, p. 19).

EGW: **No.** "Though called a 'Cushite woman' (Numbers 12:1, R.V.), the wife of Moses was a Midianite, and thus a descendant of Abraham" (*Patriarchs and Prophets*, p. 383).

BIBLE: **Yes.** "Miriam and Aaron began to talk against Moses because of his Cushite wife, for he had married a Cushite" (Numbers 12:1).

10. Were the Israelites destroyed by gluttony?

EGW: **Yes.** "God granted their desire, giving them flesh, and leaving them to eat till their gluttony produced a plague" (*Counsels on Diet and Foods*, p. 148).

BIBLE: **No.** "But while the meat was still between their teeth and before it could be consumed, the anger of the Lord burned against the people, and he struck them with a severe plague" (Numbers 11:33).

11. Did God send ravens to feed Elijah?

EGW: **No.** "There He honored Elijah by sending food to him morning and evening by an angel of heaven" (*Testimonies*, vol. 3, p. 288 written in 1873).

EGW: **Yes.** "He who fed Elijah by the brook, making a raven His messenger" (*Testimonies*, vol. 4, p. 253 written in 1876).

BIBLE: **Yes.** "I have ordered the ravens to feed you. ... The ravens brought him bread and meat" (1 Kings 17:4, 6).

12. Did Samson disobey God when he married a Philistine?

EGW: **Yes.**

> A young woman dwelling in the Philistine town of Timnath engaged Samson's affections, and he determined to make her his wife. ... The parents at last yielded to his wishes, and the marriage took place. ... The time when he must execute his divine mission — the time above all others when he should have been true to God — Samson connected himself with the enemies of Israel. ... He was placing himself in a position where he could not fulfill the purpose to be accomplished by his life. ... The wife, to obtain whom Samson had transgressed the command of God, proved treacherous to her husband. (*Patriarchs and Prophets*, pp. 562,563)

BIBLE: **No.** "Samson said to his father, 'Get her for me. She's the right one for me.' (His parents did not know this was from the Lord, who was seeking an occasion to confront the Philistines) ..." (Judges 14:3-4).

13: Did the high priest carry the blood of sacrificed animals into the Holy Place each day?

EGW: **Yes.**

> The most important part of the daily ministration was the service performed in behalf of individuals. ... By his own hand the animal was then slain, and the blood was carried by the priest into the holy place and sprinkled before the veil, behind which was the ark containing the law that the sinner had transgressed. By

this ceremony the sin was, through the blood, transferred in figure to the sanctuary. (*Patriarchs and Prophets,* p. 354)

BIBLE: **No.** Apart from the annual Day of Atonement, the priest only sprinkled blood "before the veil" in the Holy Place on two occasions: (1) when a priest sinned (Leviticus 4:3-12); (2) when the whole Israelite community sinned (Leviticus 4:13-21). Blood was never taken into the Holy Place on a daily basis when a leader sinned (Leviticus 4:22-26), nor when an individual sinned (Leviticus 4:27-35).

14. Did Christ resemble other children?

EGW: **Yes.** 1896: "He was to be like those who belonged to the human family and the Jewish race. His features were to be like those of other human beings, and he was not to have such beauty of person as to make people point him out as different from others" (*Christ Our Saviour*, p. 9, Edition 1896).

EGW: **No.** 1898: "No one, looking upon the childlike countenance, shining with animation, could say that Christ was just like other children" (*Questions on Doctrine*, p. 649, 1957). Just more of EGW's ignorance!

Bible: **Yes.** "He grew up before him like a tender shoot, and like a root out of dry ground. He had no beauty or majesty to attract us to him, nothing in his appearance that we should desire him" (Isaiah 53:2, NIV).

15. Was the man Jesus Christ truly God?

EGW: **No.** "The man Christ Jesus was not the Lord God Almighty" (Letter 32, 1899, quoted in the Seventh-day Adventist Bible Commentary, vol. 5, p. 1129).

BIBLE: **Yes.** "For to us a child is born, to us a son is given, and the government will be on his shoulders. And he will be called Wonderful Counselor, Mighty God, Everlasting Father, Prince of Peace" (Isaiah 9:6).

BIBLE: **Yes.**

> Look, he is coming with the clouds, and every eye
> will see him, even those who pierced him; and all the
> peoples of the earth will mourn because of him. So
> shall it be! Amen. "I am the Alpha and the Omega,"
> says the Lord God, "who is, and who was, and who
> is to come, the Almighty." (Revelation 1:7-8)

BIBLE: **Yes.** "Therefore God exalted him (Jesus) to the
highest place and gave him the name that is above every name"
(Philippians 2:9).

16. While tempting Jesus, did Satan claim to be the angel who had
saved Isaac from certain death?

EGW: **Yes.**

> As soon as the long fast of Christ commenced in the
> wilderness, Satan was at hand with his temptations. He
> ... tried to make Christ believe that God did not require
> Him to pass through self-denial and the sufferings He
> anticipated. ... He (Satan) also stated he was the angel
> that stayed the hand of Abraham as the knife was raised
> to slay Isaac. (*Selected Messages*, vol. 1, p. 273)

BIBLE: **No.** You may read the Bible from cover to cover and
you will not find any evidence to validate this supposed conversation
between Christ and Satan.

17. Who chose Judas to be one of Jesus' twelve disciples?

EGW: **Christ chose Judas.** "When Judas was chosen by our
Lord, his case was not hopeless" (*Testimonies,* vol. 4, p. 41).
EGW: **Disciples chose Judas.** "The disciples were anxious that
Judas should become one of their number. ... They commended him
to Jesus" (*Desire of Ages*, p. 294).

EGW: **Judas chose himself.**

> While Jesus was preparing the disciples for their ordination, one who had not been summoned urged his presence among them. It was Judas Iscariot, a man who professed to be a follower of Christ. He now came forward soliciting a place in this inner circle of disciples. ... He hoped to experience this through connecting himself with Jesus. (*Desire of Ages*, pp. 293, 717).

BIBLE: **Jesus chose Judas.** "When morning came, he called his disciples to him and chose twelve of them ... Judas Iscariot, who became a traitor. ... Then Jesus replied, 'Have I not chosen you, the Twelve? ... You did not chose me, but I chose you" (Luke 6:13-16; John 6:70; 15:16).

18. Did dogs eat Judas' remains?

EGW: **Yes.** "His weight had broken the cord by which he had hanged himself to the tree. In falling, his body had been horribly mangled, and dogs were now devouring it. His remains were immediately buried out of sight" (*Desire of Ages*, p. 722).

Bible: **No.** "So Judas threw the money into the temple and left. Then he went away and hanged himself" (Matthew 27:5, NIV).

"With the reward he got for his wickedness, Judas bought a field; there he fell headlong, his body burst open and all his intestines spilled out" (Acts 1:18, NIV).

19. Did Herod place a tattered robe on Jesus?

EGW: **Yes.** "At the Suggestion of Herod, a crown was plaited from a vine bearing sharp thorns, and this was placed upon the sacred brow, of Jesus; and an old tattered purple robe, once the garment of a king, was placed upon his noble form." (*3 Spirit of Prophecy* p.138, 1887 Edition.

"Behold Him clothed in that old purple robe" (*1 Testimonies*, p. 241). One more of the false prophetess Ellen G. White's Bible that they use to replace much of the truths in the real Bible! The words fit Ellen G. White's doctrinal agenda.

Bible: **No.** "Then Herod and his soldiers ridiculed and mocked him. Dressing him in an elegant robe, they sent him back to Pilate" (Luke 23:11, NIV).

20. Did Jesus faint three times under the Cross?

EGW: **Yes.**

> He was weak and feeble through pain and suffering, caused by the scourging and blows which he had received, yet they laid on him the heavy cross upon which they were soon to nail him. But Jesus fainted beneath the burden. Three times they laid on him the heavy cross, and three times he fainted" (*Spiritual Gifts*, vol. 1, p. 57).

BIBLE: **No.** "As they were going out, they met a man from Cyrene, named Simon, and they forced him to carry the cross" (Matthew 27:32).

BIBLE: **No.** "A certain man from Cyrene, Simon, the father of Alexander and Rufus, was passing by on his way in from the country, and they forced him to carry the cross" (Mark 15:21).

BIBLE: **No.** "As they led him away, they seized Simon from Cyrene, who was on his way in from the country, and put the cross on him and made him carry it behind Jesus" (Luke 23:26).

21. Did Satan tempt Christ after He fasted forty days?

EGW: **No.** "As soon as the long fast of Christ commenced, Satan was at hand with his temptations...Satan told Christ ...that it was not necessary for him to endure this painful hunger and death from starvation" (*Redemption of the Temptation of Christ*, p. 37. 1874 Edition).

EGW: **No.** "As soon as Christ began his fast, Satan appeared as an angel of light, and claimed to be a messenger of heaven. He told him it was not the will of God that he should suffer this pain and self-denial" (*Christ Our Saviour*, p. 45. *1 Selected Messages*, p.273).

EGW: **No.** "Forty days He was tempted of Satan" (*Early Writings*, p.155).

EGW: **Yes.** "When Jesus entered the wilderness, He was shut in by the Father's glory...But the glory departed, and He was left to battle with temptation. For forty days he fasted and prayed... Now was Satan's opportunity. Now he supposed he could overcome Christ." (*Desire of Ages*, p.118)

Bible: **Yes.** "After fasting forty days and forty nights, he was hungry." (Matthew 4:2, NIV) "The tempter came to him and said, "If you are the Son of God, tell these stones to become bread" (Matthew 4,:3 NIV).

22. Was Mary led away from the scene and Jesus' bones broken during his crucifixion?

EGW: **Yes.**

> The mother of Jesus was agonized, almost beyond endurance, and as they stretched Jesus upon the cross, and were about to fasten his hands with the cruel nails to the wooden arms, the disciples bore the mother of Jesus from the scene, that she might not hear the crashing of the nails as they were driven through the bone and muscle of his tender hands and feet" (*Spiritual Gifts*, vol. 1, p. 58, written in 1858).

EGW: **No.** "His hands stretched upon the cross; the hammer and the nails were brought, and as the spikes were driven through the tender flesh, ..." (*Desire of Ages*, p. 744, written in 1898).

For real Christians who know the Bible, she only muddied up the water, or shall I say our understanding, because God called real prophets to do the writing of the real and true Bible, and said just what God wanted them to say without Ellen G. White's additions that mean nothing!

Anyone can think up stories and additions to the Bible, but most real Christians know automatically that reading God's Word is enough for man to understand. None of us need this woman's jibber-jabber expounding on God's Word, which contains real prophets' writings. We don't need a false prophetess trying to make people believe her fictional writings! We could all add to and take away from God's Word, but I don't think this would be too smart. Revelation 22:18-19 are clear concerning adding to and taking away from the Word.

All of us should use just the Bible rather than all of the Ellen G. White writings because her writings are so imperfect and are fiction.

BIBLE: **No.**

> A large number of people followed him, including women who mourned and wailed for him. ... All those who knew him, including the women who had followed him from Galilee, stood at a distance, watching these things (the crucifixion). The women who had come with Jesus from Galilee followed Joseph and saw the tomb and how his body was laid in it. (Luke 23:27, 49, 55)

BIBLE: **No.** "Near the cross of Jesus stood his mother, his mother's sister, Mary the wife of Clopas, and Mary Magdalene" (John 19:25).

BIBLE: **No.** "These things happened so that the scriptures would be fulfilled: 'Not one of his bones will be broken'" (John 19:25, 36).

23. Did Jesus' humanity and divinity die on the Cross?

EGW: **Yes.** "Men need to understand that Deity suffered and sank under the agonies of Calvary" (*Manuscript 44,* 1898, and the *Seventh-day Adventist Bible Commentary*, vol. 7, p. 907).

EGW: **No.** "The Deity did not sink under the agonizing torture of Calvary" (Letter: 1899, quoted in the *Seventh-day Adventist Bible Commentary*, vol. 5, page 1129).

BIBLE: **Yes.** "We believe that Jesus died and rose again" (1Thessalonians 4:14).

24. Did Jesus die to give us a second probation?

EGW: **Yes.** "Death entered the world because of transgression. But Christ gave his life that man should have another trial. He did not die on the cross to abolish the law of God, but to secure for man a second probation" (*Testimonies to Ministers*, p. 134).

BIBLE: **No.** "I tell you, now is the time of God's favor, now is the day of salvation" (2 Corinthians 6:2).

"How shall we escape if we ignore such a great salvation?" (Hebrews 2:3)

"Man is destined to die once, and after that to face judgment, so Christ was sacrificed once to take away the sins of many people; and he will appear a second time, not to bear sin, but to bring salvation to those who are waiting for him" (Hebrews 9:27-28).

25. Was the atonement for sin completed at the Cross?

EGW: **No.** "Instead of ... Daniel 8:14 referring to the purifying of the earth, it was now plain that it pointed to the closing work of our High Priest in heaven, the finishing of the atonement, and the preparing of the people to abide the day of His coming" (*Testimonies,* vol. 1, p. 58).

"Jesus entered the most holy of the heavenly (sanctuary), at the end of the 2300 days of Daniel 8, in 1844, to make a final atonement for all who could be benefited by His mediation" (*Early Writings*, p. 253). Mercy for Ellen G. White. Because of her fiction writings; she will need as much as she can get!

BIBLE: **Yes.** "When he had received the drink, Jesus said, 'It is finished.' With that, he bowed his head and gave up his spirit" (John 19:30).

> But now a righteousness from God, apart from law, has been made known, to which the Law and the Prophets testify. This righteousness from God comes through faith in Jesus and [sic] fall short of God, and are justified freely by his grace through the redemption that came by Christ Jesus. God presented him as

a sacrifice of atonement, through faith in his blood. (Romans 3:21-25)

Since we have now been justified by his blood, how much more shall we be saved from God's wrath through him! For if, when we were God's enemies, we were reconciled to him through the death of his Son, how much more, having been reconciled, shall we be saved through his life! Not only is this so, but we also rejoice in God through our Lord Jesus Christ, through whom we have now received reconciliation. (Romans 5:9 11)

"Not only is this so, but we also rejoice in God through our Lord Jesus Christ, through whom we have now received reconciliation." (Romans 5:11, NIV)

26. Does the blood of Christ cancel sin?

EGW: **No.** "The blood of Christ, while it was to release the repentant sinner from the condemnation of the law, was not to cancel sin ... it will stand in the sanctuary until the final atonement" (*Patriarchs and Prophets*, p. 357).

BIBLE: **Yes.** "In him we have redemption through his blood, the forgiveness of sins" (Ephesians 1:7).

"And the blood of Jesus, his son purifies us from every sin" (1 John 1:7).

"Blessed are they whose transgressions are forgiven, whose sins are covered. Blessed is the man whose sin the Lord will never count against him" (Romans 4:7-8).

27. Are confessed sins transferred to the heavenly sanctuary by the blood of Christ?

EGW: **Yes.** "As the sins of the people were anciently transferred in figure, to the earthly sanctuary by the blood of the sin-offering, so our sins are, in fact, transferred to the heavenly sanctuary by the blood of Christ." (Great Controversy p. 266, 1886 Edition).

The biggest farce yet written by their false prophetess! This fake Bible or Ellen G. White's Bible or fiction that answers all the SDA questions because their false prophetess wrote the fictional *Great Controversy*, which was invented in her own mind to cover her SDA agenda. In my view The *Great Controversy* is the most out of reach or non-biblical book every written because it was written by the SDA false prophetess who made up things as she needed them to cover their non-biblical statements and claims , which is okay to say because this is one of the reasons God called us researchers together to put stop to this Seventh Day Adventist and Ellen G. White!

"As anciently the sins of the people were by faith placed upon the sin offering and through its blood transferred in figure to the earthly sanctuary so in the new covenant the sins of the repentant are by faith placed upon Christ and transferred, in fact, to the heavenly sanctuary" (*Great Controversy* p. 421 1911 Edition).

Bible: **No.** "But if we walk in the light, as he is in the light, we have fellowship with one another, and the blood of Jesus, his Son, purifies us from all sin" (1 John 1:7, NIV).

"In him we have redemption through his blood, the forgiveness of sins, in accordance with the riches of God's grace" (Ephesians 1:7, NIV).

The Investigative Judgment was written by Ellen G. White, the Seventh Day Adventists' false prophetess. According to our findings and the truths of the bible the SDA's people are worshiping a false prophetess.ence Revelation 22:18-19. She added to and she took away from Scripture. Why would anyone continue following such a false prophetess knowing what she has done and how she has modified the true Word of God with her scriptural commentaries. See the Seventh Day Adventist Study Bible and review her comments nearly on every page.

28. Who bears our sins?

EGW: **Satan.**

It was seen, also, that while the sin offering pointed to Christ as a sacrifice, and the high priest represented Christ as a mediator, the scapegoat typified Satan, the author of sin, upon whom the sins of the truly penitent will finally be placed. ... Christ will place all these sins upon Satan, ... so Satan ... will at last suffer the full penalty of sin (*Great Controversy*, p. 422, 485, 486).

Without the *Great Controversy*, there would be no Seventh Day Adventist Church, and this is the goal of our research and due diligence. God called us to identify the lies of the SDAs and Ellen G. White's ignorance and to alert the SDA church that they are following a Satan-driven false prophetess and that's a no-no in God's eyes. God doesn't share His glory with anybody in this case!

BIBLE: **Jesus.** "He himself (Jesus Christ) bore our sins in his body on the tree, so that we might die to sins and live for righteousness; by his wounds you have been healed" (1 Peter 2:24).

29. Does God require a trespass offering before He pardons us?

EGW: **Yes.** "You cannot make every case right, for some whom you have injured have gone into their graves, and the account stands registered against you. In these cases the best you can do is to bring a trespass offering to the altar of the Lord, and He will accept and pardon you" (*Testimonies*, vol. 5, p. 339).

BIBLE: **No.** "If we confess our sins, he is faithful and just and will forgive our sins and purify us from all unrighteousness" (1 John 1:9).

God tells you to confess your sins and you will be pardoned and purified. EGW contradicts the Bible by telling you to bring a trespass offering to be pardoned.

30. Can we say we are saved right now by Christ's grace?

EGW: **No.** "Those who accept the Saviour, however sincere their conversion, should never be taught to say or feel that they are saved. ... Those who accept Christ, and in their first confidence say,

I am saved, are in danger of trusting to themselves" (*Christ's Object Lessons*, p. 155).

BIBLE: **Yes.** "I write these things to you who believe in the name of the Son of God so that you may know that you have eternal life" (1 John 5:13).

31. Can the faith of believing parents save their children?

EGW: **Yes.**

> I know that some questioned whether the little children of even believing parents should be saved, because they have had no test of character and all must be tested and their character determined by trial. The question is asked, "How can little children have this test and trial?" I answer that the faith of the believing parents covers the children. (*Selected Messages*, vol. 3, p. 313)

BIBLE: **No.**

> If I bring a sword against that country ... and I kill its men and their animals, as surely as I live, declares the Sovereign Lord, even if these three men (Noah, Daniel and Job) were in it, they could not save their own sons or daughters. They alone would be saved. Or if I send a plague into that land and pour out My wrath upon it, ... even if Noah, Daniel and Job were in it, they could save neither son nor daughter. They would save only themselves by their righteousness. (Ezekiel 14:17-20)

BIBLE: **No.** "The soul who sins is the one who will die. The son will not share the guilt of the father, nor will the father share the guilt of the son. The righteousness of the righteous man will be credited to him, and the wickedness of the wicked will be charged against him" (Ezekiel 18:20).

BIBLE: **No.** "I will judge each of you according to his own ways" (Ezekiel 33:20).

32. Will the sins of the slave be transferred to the slave master?

EGW: **Yes.** "I saw that the slave master will have to answer for the soul of his slave whom he has kept in ignorance; and the sins of the slave will be visited upon (transferred to) the master" (*Early Writings*, p. 276).

BIBLE: **No.** "I will judge each of you according to his own ways" (Ezekiel 33:20).

"The righteousness of the righteous man will be credited to him, and the wickedness of the wicked will be charged against him" (Ezekiel 18:20).

"When I say unto the wicked, O wicked man, thou shalt surely die; if thou dost not speak to warn the wicked from his way, that wicked man shall die in his iniquity; but his blood will I require at thine hand." (Ezekiel 33:8)

"It were better for him that a millstone were hanged about his neck, and he cast into the sea, than that he should offend [cause to stumble] one of these little ones" (Luke 17:2).

33. Can ignorant slaves be saved?

EGW: **No.** "God cannot take to heaven the slave who has been kept in ignorance and degradation, knowing nothing of God or the Bible, fearing nothing but his master's lash, and holding a lower position than the brutes" (*Early Writings*, p. 276). Not in the real and true Bible!, but written by their false prophetess, Ellen G. White!

BIBLE: **Yes.** "The true light (Jesus) that gives light to every man was coming into the world" (John 1:9).

34. Can we legitimately say, "I have ceased to sin"?

EGW: **Yes.** "Christ died to make it possible for you to cease to sin, and sin is the transgression of the law" (*Review and Herald*, vol. 71, No. 35, p. 1, August 28, 1894.)

"To be redeemed means to cease from sin" (*Review and Herald*, vol. 77, No. 39, p. 1, September 25, 1900).

"Those only who through faith in Christ obey all of God's commandments will reach the condition of spinelessness in which Adam lived before his transgression. They testify to their love of Christ by obeying all his precepts" (Manuscript 122, 1901, quoted in the *Seventh-day Adventist Bible Commentary*, vol. 6, p. 1118).

"To everyone who surrenders fully to God is given the privilege of living without sin, in obedience to the law of heaven. ... God requires of us perfect obedience. We are to purify ourselves, even as he is pure. By keeping his commandments, we are to reveal our love for the Supreme Ruler of the universe" (*Review and Herald*, September 27, 1906, p. 8).

BIBLE: **No.**

> The blood of Jesus, his son, purifies us from all sin. If we claim to be without sin, we deceive ourselves and the truth is not in us. If we confess our sins, he is faithful and just and will forgive us our sins and purify us from all unrighteousness. If we claim we have not sinned, we make him out to be a liar and his word has no place in our lives. (1 John 1:8-9)

"For it is by grace you have been saved, through faith — and this not from yourselves, it is the gift of God — not by works, so that no one can boast" (Ephesians 2:8-9).

35. Will obeying the Commandments earn me God's favor?

EGW: **Yes.** "To obey the commandments of God is the only way to obtain (earn) His favor" (*Testimonies*, vol. 4, p. 28). Note: the word "earn" is a parenthetical addition by D&D, not EGW, which is still not biblical!

BIBLE: **No.** "All our righteous acts are like filthy rags" (Isaiah 64:6).

"Clearly no one is justified before God by the law, because, 'The righteous will live by faith'" (Galatians 3:11).

36. Do our obedience and faith reconcile us to God?

EGW: **Yes.** "Man, who has defaced the image of God in his soul by a corrupt life, cannot, by mere human effort, effect a radical change in himself. He must accept the provisions of the gospel; he must be reconciled to God through obedience to his law and faith in Jesus Christ" (*Testimonies*, vol. 4, p. 294).

BIBLE: **No.** "For it is by grace you have been saved, through faith — and this not from yourselves, it is the gift of God — not by works, so that no one can boast" (Ephesians 2:8-9).

"Once you were alienated from God and were enemies in your minds because of your evil behavior. But now he has reconciled you by Christ's physical body through death to present you holy in his sight, without blemish and free from accusation" (Colossians 1:21-22).

37. As a Christian, do I still stand condemned before God?

EGW: **Yes.**

> At the time the light of health reform dawned upon us, and since that time, the questions have come home every day, "Am I practicing true temperance in all things? Is my diet such as will bring me in a position where I can accomplish the greatest amount of good?" If we cannot answer these questions in the affirmative, we stand condemned before God (*Counsels on Diet and Foods*, pp. 19-20).

BIBLE: **No.** "Therefore, there is now no condemnation for those who are in Christ Jesus" (Romans 8:1).

"For God did not send his Son into the world to condemn the world, but to save the world through him. Whoever believes in him is not condemned" (John 3:17-18).

"I tell you the truth, whoever hears my word and believes him who sent me has eternal life and will not be condemned; he has crossed over from death to life" (John 5:24).

38. Must I be perfect before Christ will accept me?

EGW: **Yes.** "From what was shown me, there is a great work to be accomplished for you before you can be accepted in the sight of God" (*Testimonies*, vol. 2, p. 84).

"You have a great work to do. ... It is impossible for you to be saved as you are" (*Testimonies*, vol. 2, p. 316).

"As you are, you would mar all heaven. You are uncultivated, unrefined, and unsanctified. There is no place in heaven for such a character as you now possess. ... You are further today from the standard of Christian perfection ... than you were a few months after you had received the truth" (*Testimonies*, vol. 3, p. 465). Not biblical!

BIBLE: **No.** "Because of his great love for us, God, who is rich in mercy, made us alive with Christ even when we were dead in transgressions — it is by grace you have been saved" (Ephesians 2:4-5).

"Accept one another, then, just as Christ accepted you, in order to bring praise to God" (Romans 15:7).

"God, who knows the heart, showed that he accepted them (the Gentile converts) by giving the Holy Spirit to them, just as he did to us. He made no distinction between us and them, for he purified their hearts by faith" (Acts 15:8-9).

39. Did Jesus enter the most Holy Place of the Heavenly Temple before October 22, 1844?

EGW: **No.** "I was shown that ... the door was opened in the most holy place in the heavenly sanctuary, where the ark is, in which are contained the ten commandments. This door was not opened until the mediation of Jesus was finished in the holy place of the sanctuary in 1844.

"Jesus rose up and shut the door of the holy place, and opened the door into the most holy, and passed within the second veil, where he now stands by the ark" (*Early Writings*, p. 42). This was also written by a dead false prophetess, which makes the *Early Writings* non-biblical, so why would anyone put their faith in a dead prophetess' writings?

BIBLE: **Yes.** "The point of what we are saying is this: We do have such a high priest, who sat down at the right hand of the throne of the Majesty in heaven, and who serves in the sanctuary, the true tabernacle set up by the Lord, not by man" (Hebrews 8:1-2, written in 60 AD).

"He did not enter by means of the blood of goats and calves; but he entered the Most Holy Place once for all by his own blood, having obtained eternal redemption" (Hebrews 9:12).

40. Are the forgiven sins of the saints not blotted out until the Great day of Final Reward?

EGW: **Yes.**

> The blood of Christ, while it was to release the repentant sinner from the condemnation of the law, was not to cancel the sin; it would stand on record in the sanctuary until the final atonement. ... In the great day of final award, the dead are to be 'judged out of those things which were written in the books, according to their works' (Revelation 20:12). Then by virtue of the atoning blood of Christ, the sins of all the truly penitent will be blotted from the books of heaven. (*Patriarchs and Prophets*, p. 357)

BIBLE: **No.** "I will forgive their wickedness and will remember their sins no more" (Hebrews 8:12).

"I am he who blots out your transgressions for my own sake, and remembers your sins no more" (Isaiah 43:25).

"I will forgive their wickedness and will remember their sins no more" (Jeremiah 31:34).

41. Did Paul learn the Gospel from men in the church?

EGW: **Yes.**

Paul must receive instruction in the Christian faith and move accordingly. Christ sends him to the very disciples whom he had been so bitterly persecuting, to learn of them. ... Now Paul was in a condition to learn of those whom God had ordained to teach the truth. Christ directs Paul to His chosen servants, thus placing him in connection with His church. The very men whom Paul was purposing to destroy were to be his instructors in the very religion that he had despised and persecuted. (*Testimonies*, vol. 3, p. 430).

BIBLE: **No.**

I want you to know, brothers, that the Gospel I preached is not something that man made up. I did not receive it from any man, nor was I taught it; rather, I received it by revelation from Jesus Christ. ... I did not consult any man, nor did I go up to Jerusalem to see those who were apostles before I was, but I went immediately into Arabia and later returned to Damascus. Then after three years, I went up to Jerusalem to get acquainted with Peter and stayed with him fifteen days. I saw none of the other apostles — only James, the Lord's brother. I assure you before God that what I am writing you is no lie. (Galatians 1:11-12, 16-20)

42. What is "The Seal of God"?

EGW: **Sabbath.** "The enemies of God's law, from the ministers down to the least among them, have a new conception of truth and duty. Too late they see that the Sabbath of the fourth commandment is the seal of the living God" (*Great Controversy*, p. 640). Not biblical, and again the *Great Controversy* is not even biblical, yet the Seventh Day Adventists use this to justify their non-biblical doctrines and many of their twenty-eight fundamental beliefs. All this is ridiculous in nature and in words and deeds.

BIBLE: **Holy Spirit.** "You were marked in Him with a seal, the promised Holy Spirit" (Ephesians 1:13).

"Do not grieve the Holy Spirit of God with whom you were sealed for the day of redemption" (Ephesians 4:30).

43. Are we required to kneel every time we pray?

EGW: **Yes.**

> Where have our brethren obtained the idea that they should stand upon their feet praying to God? One who has been educated about five years in Battle Creek was asked to lead in prayer before Sister White should speak to the people. But as I beheld him standing upright upon his feet while his lips were about to open in prayer to God, my soul was stirred within me to give him an open rebuke. Calling him by name, I said, "Get down on your knees! This is the proper position always." (*Selected Messages*, book 2, p. 311)

Good grief, this *Selected Messages* is also not biblical, but it is Ellen G. White! Is anybody going to believe a dead false prophetess over the real and true Bible? Of course not!

"Both in public and private worship, it is our duty to bow down before God when we offer our petitions to Him" (*Selected Messages*, book 2, p. 311).

"To bow down when in prayer to God is the proper attitude to occupy" (*Selected Messages*, book 2, p. 312).

No: "We need not wait for an opportunity to kneel before God. We can pray and talk with the Lord wherever we may be" (*Selected Messages*, book 3, p. 266).

No: "It is not always necessary to bow upon your knees in order to pray" (*Selected Messages*, book 3, p. 267). Again, please don't believe such trash! This *Selected Messages* book is not biblical because it was written by a dead false prophetess with no hope of redemption because she added to and took away from the Bible on multiple occasions (reference Revelation 22:18-19!)

BIBLE: **No.** "But the tax collector stood at a distance. He would not even look up to heaven, but beat his breast and said, 'God have mercy on me, a sinner'" (Luke 18:13).

"And when you stand praying, if you hold anything against anyone, forgive him so that your Father in heaven may forgive you your sins" (Mark 11:25).

44. Will people be lost because their pastor is untidy?

EGW: **Yes.** "The loss of some souls at last will be traced to the untidiness of the minister" (*Selected Messages*, book 3, p. 25l).

BIBLE: **No.** "I will judge each of you according to his own ways" (Ezekiel 33:20).

"The soul who sins is the one who will die. The son will not share the guilt of the father, nor will the father share the guilt of the son. The righteousness of the righteous man will be credited to him, and the wickedness of the wicked will be charged against him" (Ezekiel 18:20).

45. Is it a sin to be sick?

EGW: **Yes.** "It is a sin to be sick; for all sickness is the result of transgression" (*Counsels on Health*, p. 37).Ellen G. White was sickly all of her life and everybody in the SDA Church knows it! She must have had many transgressions.

BIBLE: **No.** "So Satan went out from the presence of the Lord and afflicted Job with painful sores from the soles of his feet to the top of his head. ... In all this, Job did not sin" (Job 2:7, 10).

46. Will God prevent the wicked from killing his people who refuse to receive the mark of the beast?

EGW: **Yes.**

God would not suffer (allow) the wicked to destroy those who were expecting translations and who would not bow to the decree of the beast or receive his mark. I saw that if the wicked were permitted to slay the saints, Satan and all his evil host and all who hate God, would be gratified. ... The swords that were raised to kill God's people broke and fell powerless as a straw. Angels of God shielded the saints. (*Early Writings*, pp. 284, 285)

BIBLE: **No.**

I saw the souls of those who had been beheaded because of their testimony for Jesus and because of the word of God. They had not worshipped the beast or his image and had not received his mark on their foreheads or their hands. They came to life and reigned with Christ a thousand years. (Revelation 20:4)

47. Do the wicked try to repent as they experience the Seven Last Plagues?

EGW: **Yes.**

The plagues were falling upon the inhabitants of the earth. Some were denouncing God and cursing Him. Others rushed to the people of God and begged to be taught how they might escape His judgments (repentance). — Those who had not prized God's Word were hurrying to and fro, wandering from sea to sea, and from the north to the east, to seek the Word of the Lord (repentance). ... What would they not give for one word of approval from God (repentance)! But no, they must hunger and thirst on. (*Early Writings*, p. 281)

BIBLE: **No.**

They were seared by the intense heat and they cursed the name of God, who had control over these plagues, but they refused to repent and glorify Him. ... Men gnawed their tongues in agony and cursed the God of heaven because of their pains and their sores, but they refused to repent of what they had done. ... and they cursed God on account of the plague of hail, because the plague was so terrible. (Revelation 16:9-11, 21)

48. Can Satan answer prayers directed to God?

EGW: **Yes.** "Satan appeared to be by the throne, trying to carry on the work of God. I saw them (Christians) look up to the throne, and pray, 'Father, give us Thy Spirit.' Satan would then breathe upon them an unholy influence ..." (*Early Writings*, p. 56). Written by Ellen G. White, which makes all those books non-biblical, as they were written by a dead false prophetess!

BIBLE: **No.** "If you, then, though you are evil, know how to give good gifts to your children, how much more will your Father in heaven give good gifts to those who ask him!" (Matthew 7:11)

"Again, I tell you that if two of you on earth agree about anything you ask for, it will be done for you by my Father in heaven" (Matthew 18:19).

49. Will we know the exact day and hour of Christ's coming?

EGW: **Yes.** "As God has shown me in holy vision ... we heard the voice of God like many waters, which gave us the day and hour of Jesus' coming" (*Early Writings*, pp. 15, 34, 285).

BIBLE: **No.** "Therefore, keep watch, because you do not know the day or the hour" (Matthew 25:13).

"No one knows about that day or hour, not even the angels in heaven, nor the Son, but only the Father" (Matthew 24:36).

50. Does Jesus return to Earth at the stroke of midnight?

EGW: **Yes.** More ignorance from the SDA false prophetess. Reference Matthew 25:13 and Acts 1:7. "It was at midnight that God chose to deliver his people. As the wicked were mocking around them, suddenly the sun appeared, shining in his strength, and the moon stood still" (*Spiritual Gifts*, vol. 1, p. 205). More slick writings, but not biblical. This is not in the Bible and again is another Ellen G. White addition to God's real and true Bible. Reference Revelation 22:18-19.

BIBLE: **No.** "Therefore, keep watch, because you do not know the day or the hour" (Matthew 25:13).

"It is not for you to know the times or dates the Father has set by his own authority" (Acts 1:7).

51. Will the saved have wings in the resurrection?

EGW: **Yes.** "We gathered about Jesus, and just as He closed the gates of the city, the curse was pronounced upon the wicked. The gates were shut. Then the saints used their wings and mounted to the top of the wall of the city" (*Early Writings*, p. 53).

BIBLE: **No.** "Who, by the power that enables him to bring everything under his control, will transform our lowly bodies so that they will be like his glorious body" (Philippians 3:21).

"Eye hath not seen, nor ear heard, neither have entered into the heart of man, the things which God hath prepared for them that love him." (1 Corinthians 2:9)

"Delight thyself also in the Lord; and He shall give thee the desires of thine heart." (Psalm 37:4)

52. Could Jesus see through the portals of the tomb?

EGW: **No.** "The Saviour could not see through the portals of the tomb. Hope did not present to Him His coming forth from the grave a conqueror, or tell Him of the Father's acceptance of the sacrifice" (*Desire of Ages,* p. 753). This was not written in the Bible, so why did Ellen G. White say it? Because it was one more of her lies! This continues to be used to prove and justify Ellen G. White's agendas, but it's not biblical.

Bible: **Yes.** "The Son of Man must be delivered into the hands of sinful men, be crucified and on the third day be raised again" (Luke 24:7, NIV).

"Jesus answered them, 'Destroy this temple, and I will raise it again in three days.'" (John 2:19, NIV)

"The reason my Father loves me is that I lay down my life — only to take it up again." (John 10:17, NIV)

"No one takes it from me, but I lay it down of my own accord. I have authority to lay it down and authority to take it up again. This command I received from my Father." (John 10:18, NIV)

"'Yes, it is as you say,' Jesus replied. 'But I say to all of you: In the future you will see the Son of Man sitting at the right hand of the Mighty One and coming on the clouds of heaven.'" (Matthew 26:64, NIV)

53. Did Enoch think to save Sodom?

EGW: **Yes.**

> He [Enoch] did not make his abode with the wicked. He did not locate in Sodom, thinking to save Sodom. He placed himself and his family where the atmosphere would be as pure as possible. Then at times he went forth to the inhabitants of the world with his God-given message. Every visit he made to the world was painful to him. He saw and understood something of the leprosy of sin. After proclaiming his message, he always took back with him to his place of retirement some who had received the warning. Some of these became overcomers, and died before the Flood came. But some had lived so long in the corrupting influence of sin that they could not endure righteousness. (MS 42, 1900. *Seventh-day Adventist Bible Commentary*, Vol. 1, page 1087, paragraph 10.)

Bible: **No.** This statement contradicts the Bible, as there is no reference to Sodom existing before the flood.

SUMMARY

Fools rush into the SDA church and only stay until they find out that the Seventh Day Adventist Church is a *cult.* **Many in the SDA church put their faith in the church's false prophetess, Ellen G. White, and her writings, plus their non-biblical doctrine, rather than in Jesus Christ. The people in the church continually keep this dead false prophetess in their limelight, so these SDA people are the ones that I hope this book reaches with the truth.**

CHAPTER 6

THE MARK OF THE BEAST

According to Ellen G. White:

> The Sabbath will be the great test of loyalty, for it is the point of truth especially controverted. When the final test shall be brought to bear upon men, then the line of distinction will be drawn between those who serve God and those who serve Him not. While the observance of the false Sabbath in compliance with the law of the state, contrary to the fourth commandment, will be an avowal of allegiance to a power that is in opposition to God, the keeping of the true Sabbath, in obedience to Gods law, is an evidence of loyalty to the Creator. While one class, by accepting the sign of submission to earthly powers, receive the mark of the beast, the other choosing the token of allegiance to divine authority, receive the seal of God. (***The Great Controversy***, 1950, p. 605)

More of Ellen G. White's ignorance and fiction! Don't you believe it, because it is not biblical!

In other words, EGW stated *only* Saturday Sabbatarians will not receive "the mark of the beast." If you worship God on Sunday, like the early Christians did (Acts 20:7; 1 Corinthians 16:2), then you *will* receive the mark of the beast, according to EGW! ß ***Ridiculous; the Sabbath pertains to the Jews and no one else! If you are not Jewish, don't worry about what Ellen G. White writes or says, because her writings concerning many things mostly are not only dangerous, but they are not biblical, especially the ignorance of Ellen G. White concerning the truths of the Bible. Even more of her lies and fiction. This is not what the Bible said nor is it what was meant by the scriptures as written by God!***

According to Ellen G. White:

The Sabbath will be the great test of loyalty, for it is the point of truth especially controverted. When the final test shall be brought to bear upon men, ß ***(where is this located in the Bible?)*** *then the line of distinction will be drawn between those who serve God and those who serve Him not.* (ß ***This is not biblical, just more of Ellen G. White's foolishness and fiction!***)
While the observance of the false Sabbath in compliance with the law of the state, contrary to the fourth commandment, will be an avowal of allegiance to a power that is in opposition to God, the keeping of the true Sabbath, in obedience to God's law, is an evidence of loyalty to the Creator. ß(***Where is this located in the Bible?***) While one class, by accepting the sign of submission to earthly powers, receive the mark of the beast, the other choosing the token of allegiance to divine authority, receive the seal of God (*The Great Controversy*, 1950, p. 605). ß ***All this comes from the writings of Ellen G. White. Yes! It is more of the Seventh Day Adventists' and Ellen G. White's nonsense!***
Anyone who would prophecy a date that Jesus would return has to be ignorant of Matthew 22:24-25. Anyone who would do it twice may possibly not believe in the bible.
Study the material in this document and you will find that nearly all of the Seventh Day Adventist doctrines are bogus, and much of what they believe comes from Ellen G. White's writings and her agenda, which promotes herself and not the gospel of Jesus Christ.
The Seventh Day Adventists teach the gospel plus Ellen G. White, but wouldn't you think God would prefer we worship and have faith

in Him, rather than have faith in some other woman or another gospel that is perpetrated in a proven false prophetess' spoken words and false writings with her Seventh Day Adventist Study Bible? She added to the scriptures and even took away from the truths of the Bible. Yes, their own made up fiction Bible and their so-called doctrine justification, written and implemented into the scriptures that ether replace or change the truths of the Bible. Yes! *The Great Controversy,* does just that, written by the Seventh Day Adventists' false prophetess to overshadow and even change much of the meaning of the truths of the Bible!

ABOUT THE AUTHOR

The author has done something that not many have been able to do before now. He has gained pertinent outside and inside information on church doctrine and much information and knowledge from the positive and negative history of the Seventh Day Adventist Church. This research included why they support and cover up the non-biblical aspects of their church, including most of their twenty-eight fundamental beliefs and non-biblical doctrine.

As a government employee, he has a background of solving electrical, electronic, and design and construction problems. He is a licensed Journeyman and Master Electrician, worked with the Department of Justice, Bureau of Prisons as a supervisor of their electronics, and electric shops and was responsible for their communication central office. He then transferred to the hospital division of the Corps of Engineers field office, then to their regional office in San Antonio, Texas. After three years, he was asked to return to the Fort Worth District office of the Corps of Engineers in their engineering department. He replaced the district electrical engineer, where he worked until retirement in 1998. After his retirement, he founded Jim's Custom Homes, Inc., and built Large Custom Homes and Commercial buildings in the Fort Worth and Burleson areas for twenty-three years.

He has a vast background in research of many things including the design, construction, and installation of storm shelters and aircraft hangars.

Working out of the Corps of Engineers District office I also supported the design and electrical construction on three hospitals while working in the Corps of Engineer's District Office in Fort Worth, Texas, Carswell Air Force Base hospital, the Nellis Air Force Base Hospital in Las Vegas and the BAMC hospital and burn center located in San Antonio, Texas on I-35.

When he was about twelve years old, his father bought him a guitar, and he has played ever since. His wife Mary is a retired school teacher of thirty-one years. He accompanies himself and his wife on the guitar when they sing in concerts or provide musical specials in their church or other churches. Both Mary and Jim are Christians and are members of the Nazarene church.

Milton Keynes UK
Ingram Content Group UK Ltd.
UKHW010626150124
436059UK00001B/185

9 781498 494847